MILITARY MACHINES

SHIPS

BY CHARLES MARLIN

WWW.APEXEDITIONS.COM

Copyright © 2025 by Apex Editions, Mendota Heights, MN 55120. All rights reserved. No part of this book may be reproduced or utilized in any form or by any means without written permission from the publisher.

Apex is distributed by North Star Editions:
sales@northstareditions.com | 888-417-0195

Produced for Apex by Red Line Editorial.

Photographs ©: Communication Specialist 2nd Class Samantha Oblander/US Navy/DVIDS, cover; Master Sgt. Ryan Crane/US Air Force/DVIDS, 1, 8–9; Declan Barnes/US Navy, 4–5; Mass Communication Specialist 3rd Class Olympia O. McCoy/US Navy/DVIDS, 6; Photographer's Mate 1st Class Brien Aho/US Navy, 7; iStockphoto, 10–11; Naval Historical Foundation/US Naval History and Heritage Command, 12–13; Wikimedia, 14; David Buell/US Navy, 15; Mass Communication Specialist 3rd Class Nicholas V. Huynh/US Navy/DVIDS, 16–17; Shutterstock Images, 19; Sgt. Manuel A. Serrano/US Marine Corps/DVIDS, 20–21; Mass Communication Specialist 2nd Class Kaila V. Peters/US Navy/DVIDS, 22–23; LPhot Unaisi Luke/UK Ministry of Defence, 24–25, 29; Ensign Ian Tumulty/US Navy/DVIDS, 26–27

Library of Congress Control Number: 2024941299

ISBN
979-8-89250-339-6 (hardcover)
979-8-89250-377-8 (paperback)
979-8-89250-449-2 (ebook pdf)
979-8-89250-415-7 (hosted ebook)

Printed in the United States of America
Mankato, MN
012025

NOTE TO PARENTS AND EDUCATORS

Apex books are designed to build literacy skills in striving readers. Exciting, high-interest content attracts and holds readers' attention. The text is carefully leveled to allow students to achieve success quickly. Additional features, such as bolded glossary words for difficult terms, help build comprehension.

TABLE OF CONTENTS

CHAPTER 1
A FIGHT AT SEA 4

CHAPTER 2
HISTORY 10

CHAPTER 3
DIFFERENT SHIPS 16

CHAPTER 4
BATTLE GROUPS 22

COMPREHENSION QUESTIONS • 28
GLOSSARY • 30
TO LEARN MORE • 31
ABOUT THE AUTHOR • 31
INDEX • 32

CHAPTER 1

A Fight at Sea

A destroyer sails on enemy waters. It races to help fight a nearby battle. One crew member spots a **submarine** on the ship's **sonar**. It's an attack!

Sonar helps a ship's crew find things that are hidden underwater.

Submarines can move quietly underwater. They can sneak up on enemies.

The submarine heads toward the destroyer. The crew members jump into action. They fire a torpedo. It shoots from the ship's side and zooms through the water.

TORPEDOES

Torpedoes use **propellers** to move through water. Many torpedoes also have sensors. They use sound to track and hit targets. They can follow a target if it moves.

Torpedo launchers use blasts of air to shoot torpedoes from tubes.

The torpedo hits the sub and explodes. A huge splash rises into the air. The ship is safe. The crew speeds off to continue the fight.

FAST FACT
Torpedoes can travel up to 25 miles (40 km) to reach targets.

Military ships often travel about 35 miles per hour (56 km/h).

CHAPTER 2

History

Thousands of years ago, people used small wooden ships in battle. By the 1300s, many militaries used larger warships. Often, the ships had guns mounted along their sides.

In the 1600s, many warships weighed thousands of tons. They had dozens of cannons and guns.

People began building steam-powered ships in the early 1800s. By the late 1800s, most warships were made of metal. Many could fire powerful torpedoes.

FAST FACT
The first battle between two iron warships happened in the American Civil War (1861–1865).

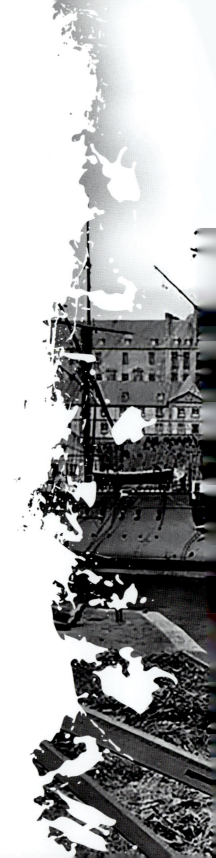

Metal ships were harder to sink than wooden ships. Their strong sides could block many attacks.

During the 1900s, ships became bigger and faster. Huge battleships fought in several wars. Later, other ships began replacing them.

In the 1900s, many ships used oil-powered engines. They could travel far without refueling.

The USS *North Carolina* was a battleship that fought in World War II (1939–1945). It was 728 feet (222 m) long.

CHANGING TYPES

From the 1860s to 1940s, many militaries **relied** on battleships. During World War II (1939–1945), airplanes began playing a bigger **role**. So, militaries focused on building ships to carry planes.

CHAPTER 3

Different Ships

Today, militaries use many types of ships. They often use cruisers and destroyers. These ships carry large **weapons**.

Cruisers (front) are often larger than destroyers (back).

Most warships carry several kinds of guns and **missiles**. They can hit enemies on land and at sea. Some shoot targets more than 23 miles (37 km) away.

SAME JOB

In the past, cruisers were faster than destroyers. They could also travel farther. Destroyers carried more weapons. They shot down enemy ships. Today, both ships do similar jobs.

Some weapons systems can fire 4,500 shots in one minute. ▶

Some ships move troops. These ships bring soldiers to faraway battles. Other ships carry planes or helicopters. On aircraft carriers, planes can take off and land.

Some ships carry smaller boats. These small boats take troops onto land.

FAST FACT
Aircraft carriers can hold more than 75 planes.

CHAPTER 4

BATTLE GROUPS

Sometimes, warships sail alone. But they often travel in groups called fleets. They work together on **missions**.

One fleet may include dozens of ships.

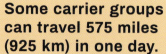
Some carrier groups can travel 575 miles (925 km) in one day.

For example, several ships often sail with aircraft carriers. Some of the ships carry supplies. Others protect the carriers. They find and fight off enemies.

CARRIER GROUPS

Aircraft carriers are huge ships. But they don't have many weapons. So, they are common targets for enemy attacks. Cruisers and destroyers help them stay safe.

Each ship has many crew members. Some members communicate with other ships. They use computers and radios to send important information. **Engineers** fix and maintain the ship. They keep it working.

FAST FACT
Ships can stay at sea for months.

Some destroyers have about 300 crew members on board.

27

COMPREHENSION QUESTIONS

Write your answers on a separate piece of paper.

1. Write a few sentences describing the main ideas of Chapter 4.

2. Which type of warship do you think is the most interesting? Why?

3. When were the first steam-powered ships built?
   - A. the early 1800s
   - B. the late 1800s
   - C. the 1900s

4. Why might cruisers and destroyers do similar jobs today?
   - A. They have similar weapons and speed now.
   - B. Their old jobs were not important.
   - C. They can't do their jobs alone.

5. What does **protect** mean in this book?

*Some of the ships carry supplies. Others **protect** the carriers. They find and fight off enemies.*

- **A.** blow something up
- **B.** keep something safe
- **C.** make something leave

6. What does **communicate** mean in this book?

*Some members **communicate** with other ships. They use computers and radios to send important information.*

- **A.** carry many missiles
- **B.** form large carrier groups
- **C.** send and receive messages

Answer key on page 32.

GLOSSARY

engineers
People who use math and science to solve problems.

missiles
Objects that are shot or launched as weapons.

missions
Tasks or plans with specific goals.

propellers
Spinning blades that move vehicles through water.

relied
Used or needed something.

role
A part in a plan that involves a bigger group.

sonar
A system that uses sound waves to measure distances and find objects underwater.

submarine
A ship that can stay deep underwater for a long time.

weapons
Things that are used to cause harm.

BOOKS

Hustad, Douglas. *US Navy Equipment and Vehicles*. Minneapolis: Abdo Publishing, 2022.

Storm, Ashley. *US Navy*. Mendota Heights, MN: Apex Editions, 2023.

Vonder Brink, Tracy. *The United States Navy*. North Mankato, MN: Capstone Publishing, 2021.

ONLINE RESOURCES

Visit **www.apexeditions.com** to find links and resources related to this title.

ABOUT THE AUTHOR

Charles Marlin is an author, editor, and avid cyclist. He lives in rural Iowa.

INDEX

A
aircraft carriers, 20–21, 24–25
American Civil War, 12

B
battleships, 14–15

C
crew members, 4, 6, 8, 26
cruisers, 16, 18, 25

D
destroyers, 4, 6, 16, 18, 25

F
fleets, 22

M
missiles, 18
missions, 22

P
propellers, 7

S
sensors, 7
sonar, 4
submarine, 4, 6, 8

T
targets, 7–8, 18, 25
torpedoes, 6–8, 12

W
weapons, 16, 18, 25
World War II, 15

ANSWER KEY:
1. Answers will vary; 2. Answers will vary; 3. A; 4. A; 5. B; 6. C